HOW AM I TEACHING?
Forms and Activities for
Acquiring Instructional Input

by
Maryellen Weimer
Joan L. Parrett
Mary-Margaret Kerns

Magna Publications, Inc.
Madison, WI

© 1988 Magna Publications, Inc.
Revised editon, second printing

Cover design by Tamara L. Cook
Interior design by Darcy Kamps

Magna Publications, Inc.
2718 Dryden Drive
Madison, WI 53704

800/433-0499
608/246-3597 (fax)

AN INTRODUCTION

Instructional effectiveness can be improved with specific input describing the impact of current instructional strategies. Too often instructors think about assessments of instructional effectiveness only in terms of end-of-course evaluation by students. That input has value, but it also has limitations. It is available after a course has concluded, thus foreclosing the option of incorporating changes during the semester. Frequently, end-of-course evaluations are summative — meaning they provide data that are comparative (ranks instructors against each other or norms) and judgmental (for example, course made interesting by instructor). Aspects of teaching are described abstractly (for example, instructor's attitude towards teaching the course), so the evaluations are based on inference and that makes it hard to determine what it is that one does that results in the ratings. Research has documented that data like this are only modestly, if at all, effective in improving instruction.

There are better ways of using data from students, others, and even oneself to positively affect instructional quality. This catalogue of forms and activities introduces instructors to a variety of these possibilities. Some of them are designed to assess specific aspects of instruction. Others propose unique ways of involving colleagues in assessment efforts. Still others propose evaluation activities that involve students. All aim to produce valuable information for instructors dedicated to providing students quality educational experiences and all are designed for use "during" a course.

The catalogue can also serve as an idea source. If something here sparks another idea or possible adaptation of one of the forms proposed, that idea can be pursued and used to benefit the individual's instruction. The point is that a variety of ways exist to obtain useful input about instruction. When evaluation occurs under an instructor's aegis and control, it can be tailor-made to fit the instructional situation. A corollary conclusion is that efforts to improve instruction ought to be continual. What works in one course, one semester may or may not be effective next time around. Instructional effectiveness is a challenge that is never permanently met.

If you like to "shop" in catalogues by browsing, do so here. Each form is prefaced with a sheet which summarizes its purpose, provides advice on administration, and proposes ways of interpreting the results. If you would like to access the material more systematically, two charts summarizing the contents follow this introduction. Locate the individual forms in the catalogue by using the index immediately following the tables. Forms in the catalogue may be copied by individual instructors who wish to use them as part of their efforts to improve instructional effectiveness.

FORM:

HOW AM I TEACHING?   *Forms and Activities for Acquiring Instructional Input*

DOES THIS DESCRIBE YOU?	RECOMMENDED FORM:
You need new ideas, fresh vision, new approaches for a course you've taught countless times before.	Open-Ended Questionnaire
Previous evaluation results are spotty, inconsistent, and you can't precisely put your finger on what needs to be changed.	Specifically, What Needs Improvement? (Student Version)
You'd like input about your instruction from somebody other than students, but asking a colleague to come to class and having no idea what they might say about the instruction is cause for trepedation.	A Made-to-Order Form for Instructional Observation (Peer Version)
You've given the students a chance to offer feedback about the course, and now you'd like to encourage them to assume part of the responsibility for making the classroom climate better.	Specifically, What Needs Improvement? (Instructor Version)
Evaluation activities that aim to provide feedback to improve instruction ought to offer the opportunity to find out what you really want to know about your teaching, but how in the world do you phrase the items and format the instrument?	A Made-to-Order Form for Instructional Observation (Peer Version and/or Student Version) Open-Ended Questionaire
You're curious about a numer of very mechanical aspects of presenting material, like how you clarify content, what aspects of your nonverbal delivery keep students interested and attentive. In other words, you're interested in a real nuts and bolts description of your lecturing techniques.	Teacher Behaviors Inventory
You haven't been trained to teach and learned to do it pretty much by doing it. You haven't ever given it much thought, but do realize that if somebody asked you for a detailed description of your teaching style, you'd be hard pressed to prepare one. You can see value in being a bit more "instructionally aware."	How Do You Teach?

DOES THIS DESCRIBE YOU?	RECOMMENDED FORM:
It crosses your mind that the course materials you use (like a syllabus, skeleton lecture outlines, study guides, assignment checklists) are included because you believe they support and supplement what you are trying to accomplish in the course. However, you've never really tried to assess how effective they are in achieving that goal.	Course Materials Review (Student and/or Peer Version)
You are tired by all the hoopla surrounding student evaluation and peer review. Isn't there something you can do on your own that can help you get a handle on what's happening in class?	Instructor Self-Evaluation Form How Do You Teach?
Your find the descriptions of teaching on most evaluation instruments vague and abstract, often describing elusive qualitites of one's personality. You wish somebody would just tell you what instructors need to do in order to be effective.	Teacher Behavior Inventory
The environment in your class concerns you. You wonder if students find it constructive, positive—an atmosphere that contributes to their learning endeavors.	Classroom Environment Inventory
You hear and read a lot about professional burnout. In quiet moments you wonder if maybe you. . .	Instructor Self-Evaluation
You need specific illustrations of what it is you do when, for example, students find themselves motivated to participate in your course.	Open-Ended Quesitonaire
So, how do you really look when you are teaching? You hear yourself day after day and see yourself, sort of—but how does it look from the third row?	Self or Colleague Analysis of Videotaped Teaching Sample
You've got the message that there are a lot of forms in this catalogue. A number of them sound intriguing. You wish somebody would make a recommendation about where to begin.	How Do You Teach?
Something about this class doesn't feel right. The students don't seem to be with you. Sometimes they appear to share a joke nobody has let you in on. You may be reading too much into the situation. What you have are intangible feelings—you need something more concrete.	Classroom Environment Inventory
You're puzzled, just what kind of a learning environment do students want? You'd love to have them describe the ideal classroom experience for them.	Classroom Environment Inventory

FORM:

HOW AM I TEACHING? *Forms and Activities for Acquiring Instructional Input*

FORM NAME	DESCRIPTION	WHO PROVIDES INPUT	VALUE	LIMITATIONS
Open-Ended Questionaire	A collection of focused questions soliciting answers for more than one word	Students	Excellent source of ideas Pinpoint and/or elaborate problems	Produces a plethora of details which make concise conclusions more difficult to reach Requires time for the student to complete
Self or Colleague Analysis of Videotaped Teaching Sample	For use when reviewing a videotaped sample of teaching Focuses attention of viewer on various behavioral aspects of teaching	Instructor or colleague	Focuses the video feedback on analysis of identifiable teaching behaviors Encourages comprehensive confrontation with the teaching self	Taped teaching samples capture only part of the action in the complex classroom milieu The presence of the camera may affect the teaching performance—making its representativesness questionable
Teacher Behaviors Inventory	An inventory of 60 items, each referring to a specific classroom teaching behavior that has been found to strongly correlate with student evaluation of overall teaching effectiveness	Students	Facilitates improvement by describing teaching behaviors; what teachers *do*, not what they *are* Provides good concrete input, focused on the presentational aspects of instruction	Not as valuable in discussion seminar or tutorial settings

FORM NAME	DESCRIPTION	WHO PROVIDES INPUT	VALUE	LIMITATIONS
How Do You Teach?	A simple list of questions that aims to develop instructional awareness—make faculty members aware of how they teach at a very behavioral level	Instructor	Forces descriptions of teaching that are very concrete and specific Makes instructional alterations easier to implement because instructors know what they are changing from and to	Relies on self-assessment which means potential perceptual distortion Encourages consideration of teaching behaviors minus the context in which they occur
Specifially, What Needs Improvement? (Student Version)	Combines scales and comments so as to help the faculty member identify specific aspects of instruction where improvement activities ought to focus	Students	By comparing ranking on items, the relative merit of instructional practices can be assessed Solicits suggestions for improvement in the given areas	Requires time to complete Quality of feedback depends on concerned, conscientious student response
Specifically, What Needs Improvement? (Instructor Version)	Uses scales and space for comments to provide the instructor an opportunity to give students feedback about the class performance	Instructor	Reinforces the idea that classroom climate is not exclusively a faculty responsibility Can be used to improve students' classroom behaviors	Difficult to communicate criticism to a class constructively Requires instructor courage to address behavioral issues so explicilty

FORM NAME	DESCRIPTION	WHO PROVIDES INPUT	VALUE	LIMITATIONS
Instructor Self-Evaluation Form	Uses 11 sets of four items each to help a faculty member gain insight into: the adequacy of classroom procedures, enthusiasm for teaching, knowledge of the subject matter, stimulation of students, and relations with them	Instructor	Is a challenging and frustrating task that forces confrontation with the instructional self Is less threatening because the results need not be shared, hence honest answers are possible	Any analysis of self is subject to bias (both in the positive and negative directions)
A Made-to-Order Form for Instuctional Observation (Peer Version)	The instrument itself is blank Instructors select items from categorized pools representing aspects of teaching from which they could acqurie feedback—in this case, from a colleague	Colleague	Instructor obtains feedback in areas of interest Items describe aspects of teaching which can be observed Colleagues observe instruction knowing what to look for	Self-selection process may preclude acquisition of feedback in areas where it is warranted Colleagues tend toward leniency in their evaluation of each other
A Made-to-Order Form for Instructional Observation (Student Version)	Same instrument as above, only in this case it is assembled by students and given to the class to complete	Students	The first and second values from the peer version of this form	The first limitation from the peer version of the form applies here
Course Materials Review (Peer Version)	Solicits input about materials used to support and supplement class content	Colleague	Provides feedback about an aspect of instruction infrequently assessed	Generating a set of evaluative criteria applicable and relevant to the many individualized forms of course materials is difficult

FORM NAME	DESCRIPTION	WHO PROVIDES INPUT	VALUE	LIMITATIONS
Course Materials Review (Student Version)	A modified version of the peer version solicits the same input from students	Students	Gets input from primary consumers of the course materials Also, provides feedback about an infrequently assessed aspect of instruction	Same as peer version of this form
Classroom Environment Inventory	Assess student's or instructor's perceptions of seven dimensions of the actual classroom or preferred classroom environment	Students and instructor	Gives an instructor input on important intangibles that often influence the kind and quality of student learning experiences Can be used to compare the way an environment is with the way students/ instructor would like it to be	Not suitable for use in lecture or laboratory courses

INDEX OF INVENTORIES

SECTION ONE

CLASSROOM ENVIRONMENT INVENTORY

F O R M :
CLASSROOM ENVIRONMENT INVENTORY

PURPOSE: This instrument was developed to give instructors input on the actual environment within a class, how conducive that atmosphere is to learning. No one questions that the context in which learning takes place influences directly the kind and quality of learning that occurs. Most instructors work to create a constructive and positive classroom environment. This form offers input as to how well an instructor is accomplishing this objective. Moreover, the form can also be used to give an instructor input on the kind of classroom environment the students prefer. Knowing something about the environment students prefer and knowing something about their reaction to the actual environment in this class give the instructor a clear sense of where changes might need to be made. The questionnaire is designed for use in small classes, seminars, or tutorials. It is not suitable for rating lecture or laboratory classes.

ADMINISTRATION: Distribute copies of the form to students, explaining why you are interested in this information and what you intend to do with the results. The version of the form that follows includes instructions if the form is to be used to assess student reactions to the actual environment of a given course. If you wish to use the form to get input on the environment students "prefer," change the directions to read "The purpose of this questionnaire is to find out your opinions about the classroom environments you "prefer." Indicate your opinion... ." Also adjust the scale descriptions to read "that it describes the classroom environment you prefer." As with other forms in this collection, interesting comparisons can be made if the instructor completes the form along with the students.

INTERPRETATION: Following the instrument are scoring instructions. They should be consulted later if you intend to complete the form yourself. **Do not read further if you intend to use the form.**
After you and the students have completed the instrument, consult the scoring sheet. **Note first that the numbers of some of the items on the scoring sheet are underlined.** Those items are worded negatively, which means they must be scored by reversing the scale. The second formula in Step 1 does this for you— allowing you then to interpret all the scores on a single scale.
Following the instructions on the scoring sheet, go ahead and score the individual items. We recommend against calculating overall averages

for the individual categories of the instrument. Rather, instructors are encouraged to look at the categories, noting which ones they scored highly on or regard as especially important aspects of the instructional environment. Student assessments in those areas might be more important and relevant in light of the instructor's objectives or course goals. Results that compare students' assessment of the actual environment and their preferred classroom environments should also be looked at for general trends and major differences. Instructors should spend time considering or discussing with students ways the environment in the class might be changed. What could the instructor do differently? What could the students change?

The form itself offers input about the classroom environment in seven different areas. These are listed and defined on the scoring sheet.

SOURCE: This instrument was developed by Barry J. Fraser, David F. Treagust and Norman C. Dennis of Western Australian Institute of Technology. Research describing the development and validation of the instrument appears in *"Studies in Higher Education,"* Vol. 11, No. 1, 1986. The instrument is reprinted here with their permission.

CLASSROOM ENVIRONMENT INVENTORY

Directions: The purpose of this questionnaire is to find out your opinions about the class you are attending right "now." The questionnaire assesses your opinion about what this class is "actually like." Indicate your opinion about each questionnaire statement by writing:

SA if you strongly agree that it describes what this class is actually like.
A if you agree that it describes what this class is actually like.
D if you disagree that it describes what this class is actually like.
SD if you strongly disagree that it describes what this class is actually like.

_____ 1. The instructor considers students' feelings.

_____ 2. The instructor talks rather than listens.

_____ 3. The class is made up of individuals who don't know each other well.

_____ 4. The students look forward to coming to classes.

_____ 5. Students know exactly what has to be done in our class.

_____ 6. New ideas are seldom tried out in this class.

_____ 7. All students in the class are expected to do the same work, in the same way, and in the same time.

_____ 8. The instructor talks individually with students.

_____ 9. Students put effort into what they do in class.

_____ 10. Each student knows the other members of the class by their first names.

_____ 11. Students are dissatisfied with what is done in the class.

_____ 12. Getting a certain amount of work done is important in this class.

_____ 13. New and different ways of teaching are seldom used in this class.

_____ 14. Students are generally allowed to work at their own pace.

_____ 15. The instructor goes out of his/her way to help students.

_____ 16. Students 'clockwatch' in this class.

_____ 17. Friendships are made among students in this class.

_____ 18. After the class, the students have a sense of satisfaction.

_____ 19. The group often gets sidetracked instead of sticking to the point.

_____ 20. The instructor thinks up innovative activities for students to do.

_____ 21. Students have a say in how class time is spent.

_____ 22. The instructor helps each student who is having trouble with the work.

_____ 23. Students in this class pay attention to what others are saying.

_____ 24. Students don't have much chance to get to know each other in this class.

_____ 25. Classes are a waste of time.

_____ 26. This is a disorganized class.

_____ 27. Teaching approaches in this class are characterized by innovation and variety.

_____ 28. Students are allowed to choose activities and how they will work.

_____ 29. The instructor seldom moves around the classroom to talk with students.

_____ 30. Students seldom present their work to the class.

_____ 31. It takes a long time to get to know everybody by his/her first name in this class.

_____ 32. Classes are boring.

_____ 33. Class assignments are clear so everyone knows what to do.

_____ 34. The seating in this class is arranged in the same way each week.

_____ 35. Teaching approaches allow students to proceed at their own pace.

_____ 36. The instructor isn't interested in students' problems.

_____ 37. There are opportunities for students to express opinions in this class.

_____ 38. Students in this class get to know each other well.

_____ 39. Students enjoy going to this class.

_____ 40. This class seldom starts on time.

_____ 41. The instructor often thinks of unusual class activities.

_____ 42. There is little opportunity for a student to pursue his/her particular interest in this class.

_____ 43. The instructor is unfriendly and inconsiderate toward students.

_____ 44. The instructor dominates class discussions.

_____ 45. Students in this class aren't very interested in getting to know other students.

_____ 46. Classes are interesting.

_____ 47. Activities in this class are clearly and carefully planned.

_____ 48. Students seem to do the same type of activities every class.

_____ 49. It is the instructor who decides what will be done in class.

Scoring the Classroom Environment Inventory

STEP 1:   Note the bold items listed in the categories which appear after Step 2. Determine and use the appropriate formula for calculation.

For non-bold items, use this formula:
Number of students who mark "strongly agree"   _____ x 5 =_____
Number of students who mark "agree"   _____ x 4 =_____
Number of students who mark "disagree"   _____ x 2 =_____
Number of students who mark "strongly disagree" _____ x 1 =_____
Number of omitted or invalid marks   _____ x 3 =_____
                    FREQUENCY TOTAL =   _____
                    SCORE TOTAL =   _____
                    ITEM AVERAGE = SCORE TOTAL/FREQUENCY TOTAL

For bold items, use this formula:
Number of students who mark "strongly agree"   _____ x 1 =_____
Number of students who mark "agree"   _____ x 2 =_____
Number of students who mark "disagree"   _____ x 4 =_____
Number of students who mark "strongly disagree" _____ x 5 =_____
Number of omitted or invalid marks   _____ x 3 =_____
                    FREQUENCY TOTAL =   _____
                    SCORE TOTAL =   _____
                    ITEM AVERAGE = SCORE TOTAL/FREQUENCY TOTAL

STEP 2:   Use the worksheet below to record item averages in each of the instrument's seven categories.

PERSONALIZATION — emphasizes opportunities for students to interact with the instructor and the instructor's concern for students' personal welfare.

Item   1 Item average _____
Item   8 Item average _____
Item 15 Item average _____
Item 22 Item average _____
ITEM 29 Item average _____
Item 36 Item average _____
ITEM 43 Item average _____

INVOLVEMENT — assesses extent to which students participate actively and attentively in class discussion and activities.

ITEM 2 Item average _____
Item   9 Item average _____
ITEM 16 Item average _____
Item 23 Item average _____
ITEM 30 Item average _____
Item 37 Item average _____
ITEM 44 Item average _____

STUDENT COHESIVENESS — looks at the extent to which students know, help, and are friendly toward each other.

ITEM 3 Item average _____
Item 10 Item average _____
Item 17 Item average _____
ITEM 24 Item average _____
ITEM 31 Item average _____
Item 38 Item average _____
ITEM 45 Item average _____

SATISFACTION — measures the degree of enjoyment of classes.

Item   4 Item average _____
ITEM 11 Item average _____
Item 18 Item average _____
ITEM 25 Item average _____
ITEM 32 Item average _____
Item 39 Item average _____
Item 46 Item average _____

TASK ORIENTATION — considers the extent to which class activities are clear and well-organized.

Item   5 Item average _____
Item 12 Item average _____
ITEM 19 Item average _____
ITEM 26 Item average _____
ITEM 33 Item average _____

ITEM 40 Item average _____
Item 47 Item average _____

INNOVATION — to what extent does the instructor plan new and unusual class activities, teaching techniques, and assignments?
ITEM 6 Item average _____
Item 13 Item average _____
Item 20 Item average _____
Item 27 Item average _____
ITEM 34 Item average _____
Item 41 Item average _____
ITEM 48 Item average _____

INDIVIDUALIZATION — asks to what extent students are allowed to make decisions and are treated differentially according to ability, interest, and rate of working.
ITEM 7 Item average _____
Item 14 Item average _____
Item 21 Item average _____
Item 28 Item average _____
Item 35 Item average _____
Item 42 Item average _____
Item 49 Item average _____

SECTION TWO

COURSE
MATERIALS
REVIEW
(Peer Version)

FORM:
COURSE MATERIALS REVIEW (Peer Version)

PURPOSE: Course materials communicate important information about course content, policies, and procedures and, in addition, convey messages about the atmosphere of the course and the instructor's attitude. Time can profitably be spent assessing course materials alone or with the aid of an objective outsider. Because not all messages conveyed in course materials are obvious (especially to the person who has prepared them), the quality of the review is likely to be enhanced with input from others. Fellow faculty members can offer valuable insights about course materials.

ADMINISTRATION: Colleagues can review materials at almost any point in a course and what they are given to review depends very much on the materials used. The following list is not inclusive but does include examples of course materials that might profitably be reviewed. Disregard items that are not relevant; add others that might be.

Course syllabus
Written descriptions of assignments (if not included on the syllabus)
Exams (an ungraded and graded copy)
Textbook(s)
Handouts that elaborate or supplement course content
Supplementary reading lists
Lecture outlines provided to students
Study questions/review materials
Visual materials
Individually developed materials

Because course materials are idiosyncratic— put together by individuals for use in widely differing instructional settings— not all the relevant inquiries may be listed. Colleagues should be encouraged to offer assessments in other areas if those seem appropriate.

When sharing course materials with a colleague, it is best to provide some background. What are your major goals in the course? How do you hope to have these materials help you accomplish these goals and objectives? When in the course do you use the materials? Do you provide background commentary in class? Answers to these questions put course materials in context and make it easier for a colleague reviewer to gauge their effectiveness.

INTERPRETATION: We recommend using a completed version of the form as the basis for a discussion about the materials. Colleague assessments should always be illustrated with examples. The basis for the conclusion needs to be pointed out in the materials. And remember, the colleague's assessment is really only the opinion of one person— a qualified person, but still possibly not right or representative. For this reason, you may consider using the student version of this form as well.

SOURCE: This instrument was developed by the authors. It may be copied, altered, or adapted by instructors using the form to acquire instructional input.

COURSE MATERIALS REVIEW
(Peer Version)

This form contains descriptions that should be helpful in judging the instructional materials you are reviewing. Please indicate the extent to which you would agree or disagree with each statement pertaining to course materials.

SA = strongly agree
 A = agree
SD = strongly disagree
 D = disagree
NA = not applicable

COURSE SYLLABUS

_____ Identifies instructional resources like books, films, and guest speakers

_____ Outlines the sequence of topics to be covered

_____ Describes evaluation procedures

_____ Includes a class or activity schedule or calendar

_____ Lists major assignments and due dates

_____ Contains information about the faculty member, i.e., name, office address, office hours, phone number

_____ Includes a statement or description of course objectives

_____ Is structured so that the information is clear and easily understood

_____ Is neatly typed without spelling or grammatical errors

ASSIGNMENTS (as they appear on the syllabus or in written descriptions elsewhere)

_____ Produce meaningful and challenging learning experiences

_____ Include a variety of activities that are responsive to varying student interests, abilities, and learning styles

_____ Are appropriate to course objectives and content level

_____ Are spaced at appropriate intervals in the course

_____ Are challenging but not overburdensome

_____ Prepare students for more complex courses in this subject area

HANDOUTS

_____Are relevant additions and/or elaborations of course content

_____Are structured so that the content is clearly communicated to readers

_____Are neat and minus spelling and grammatical errors

EXAMS

An Ungraded Copy:

_____Contains content consistent with course objectives — in other words, the instructor is evaluating students on what he/she believes they ought to be able to do or know

_____Contains items written so that the intent of the questions is clear and explicit

_____Uses questions in which what the question asks is clearly understood

_____Covers manageable amounts of material in terms of time allocated for studying it

_____Is too long, given the time limit of the exam period

_____Requires analysis and application of content, as opposed to regurgitation of details

A Graded Copy:

_____Includes written comments that give some feedback about both right and wrong answers

_____Presents written comments that are clear and readable

_____Includes some explanation of how the instructor calculated the exam score

TEXTBOOK(S)

_____Is/Are appropriate to course level

_____Is/Are clearly related to course objectives

_____Is/Are generally acceptable in terms of departmental standards

_____Present(s) content in a systematic and logical order so as to enhance the understanding of someone unfamiliar with the topic (Note: assess content order based on the sequence the instructor has assigned it)

_____Present(s) material interestingly so as to encourage reading

_____Supplementary Reading Lists

_____Contains relevant and current material

_____Supplements course content

_____Includes content that is challenging yet not inappropriately difficult

_____Specifies location of supplementary materials

_____Includes information to direct reading in terms of its relationship to course content

_____Lecture Outlines (provided for students)

_____Communicates a sense of proportion and detail that is consistent with content

_____Provides enough information to assist the notetaking process without making taking notes unnecessary

_____Includes space for students to write additional information

_____Is/Are enhanced by lecture presentations in class

STUDY QUESTIONS/REVIEW MATERIALS

_____Prepare one to perform successfully on exams (compare with exams)

_____Cover content that is covered on the exam

_____Are designed so that their completion facilitates student retention and understanding

_____Do not force students to focus on large quantities of material that are irrelevant to exam content

_____Provide adequate opportunity to practice problem-solving skills

_____Visual Materials (as in prepared slides and transparencies)

_____Illustrate aspects of the content that are enhanced by visual representation

_____Are clear and "graphically" illustrate the content

_____Include written elaborations that are clear and easily read

_____Can be seen and read with ease everywhere in the classroom

_____Contain manageable amounts of material, so excessive amounts of time are not required to copy down the material

OVERALL CONCLUSIONS

_____Compared with other course materials you have seen, these are better than average

_____As demonstrated by these materials, the content selected for inclusion in this course is appropriate and justifiable

_____These materials communicate an appropriate level of instructor preparation and concern

OTHER COMMENTS AND/OR ELABORATIONS:

SECTION
THREE

COURSE
MATERIALS
REVIEW
(*Student Version*)

FORM:
COURSE MATERIALS REVIEW (Student Version)

PURPOSE: Like the preceding Peer Version of this instrument, this form is premised on the assumption that course materials play a key role in the accomplishment of course objectives. Acquiring input as to their effectiveness is both legitimate and necessary. Colleagues can and ought to provide part of that assessment; the consumers of these course materials can and ought to provide the other part. This version of the form offers a means of soliciting student input about course materials. As with other forms in this packet, the primary objective is to provide input that will help an instructor increase the effectiveness of these instructional devices.

ADMINISTRATION: The form will need individual adjustments before it is used. In the first place, it is incomplete. Course objectives need to be incorporated on the form. Do not omit this step. Course objectives in this case provide the criteria against which the course materials are to be assessed. Moreover, their inclusion can serve to reinforce the relevance and propriety of the course goals. It's another opportunity for students to encounter and contemplate them. Second, the form is intended to evaluate those materials used in the course. For example, if handouts are not used, delete that section from the inventory. There may be other materials used for which items need to be generated.

Students will probably provide the best assessment of materials near the end of the course. They will have more experience using the materials than at some point earlier in the course.

INTERPRETATION: The form is constructed so that calculating means and standard deviations is not easily possible. That is by design. As with some other forms in this packet, this instrument has not been empirically tested — numbers generated off of it would be suspect. The point of the student input is to stimulate analysis and reflection directed toward course materials. It may be time to consider making some changes — this data can help to focus and direct those alterations.

Students are best qualified in this case to comment on how these materials helped or hindered accomplishment of course objectives. That is only part of the input an instructor needs. Colleagues can assess these materials in terms of content propriety. This is why we encourage use of both versions of this form.

We also strongly recommend discussing the results with students — especially if their input provokes questions. Ask them! Input about changes, adaptations, and alterations you may be considering can also be solicited from students.

SOURCE: This instrument was developed by the authors. It may be copied, altered, or adapted by instructors using the form to acquire instructional input.

COURSE MATERIALS REVIEW
(Student Version)

INSTRUCTIONS: Your instructor is requesting evaluative input as to the effectiveness of the supplementary materials (syllabus, assignments, handouts, textbooks, etc.) used in the course. Instructors use these materials to help accomplish the course objectives. Review the objectives for the course (listed below) and then "grade" the course materials listed and described on the form. Your instructor evaluates the materials you submit. Now, the tables are turned — "grade" the materials your instructor uses in the course. Assign an overall letter grade (A, B, C, D, or F) in each area and then "+" or "−" to the items listed beneath it. Assign + if the course material under consideration accomplishes the objectives very well, assign a if the objectives are accomplished but without any special distinction, and use a − when the course material does not accomplish the objectives. In those cases, if you think it might be unclear to the instructor why the material is ineffective, include a sentence that explains your objectives on the back.

COURSE OBJECTIVES

COURSE SYLLABUS: **OVERALL LETTER GRADE**_____

_____Identifies instructional resources like books, films, and guest speakers

_____Describes evaluation procedures

_____Outlines the sequence of topics to be covered

_____Includes a class or activity schedule or calendar

_____Lists major assignments and due dates

_____Contains information about the faculty member, i.e., name, office address, office hours, phone number

_____Includes a statement of description of course objectives

_____Is structured so that the information is clear and easily understood

_____Is neatly typed without spelling or grammatical errors

ASSIGNMENTS: **OVERALL LETTER GRADE**_____

_____Produce meaningful and challenging learning experiences

_____Include a variety of activities that are responsive to varying student interests, abilities, and learning styles

_____Are appropriate to course objectives and content level

_____Are spaced at appropriate intervals in the course

_____Are challenging but not overburdensome

_____Prepare students for more complex courses in this subject area

_____Are given with ample time to complete them

HANDOUTS: **OVERALL LETTER GRADE**_____

_____Are relevant additions and/or elaborations of course content

_____Are structured so that the content is clearly communicated to readers

_____Are neat and minus spelling and grammatical errors

_____Are distributed with appropriate background so their relationship to course content and objectives is clear

EXAMS: OVERALL LETTER GRADE_____

_____Contain content consistent with course objectives — in other words, the instructor is evaluating students on what he/she believes they ought to be able to do or know

_____Contains items written so that the intent of the questions is clear and explicit

_____Cover manageable amounts of material in terms of time allocated for studying it

_____Are too long, given the time limit of the exam period

_____Require analysis and application of content, as opposed to regurgitation of details

_____When graded, include written comments that give some feedback about both right and wrong answers

_____Returned exams include written comments that are clear and readable

_____When graded, contain some explanation of how the instructor calculated the exam score

TEXTBOOK(S):   OVERALL LETTER GRADE_____

_____Is/Are not too easy or difficult

_____Is/Are clearly related to course objectives

_____Present(s) content in a systematic and logical order that makes it easy to understand the material

_____Present(s) material interestingly so as to encourage reading

_____Is/Are used in ways that show the relationship between book content and class content

SUPPLEMENTAL READING LISTS: OVERALL LETTER GRADE_____

_____Contain material that seems relevant to the course

_____Supplement course content

_____Include content that is challenging yet not inappropriately difficult

_____Contain materials that are easy to locate and convenient to use

_____Include information to direct reading in terms of its relationship to course content

LECTURE OUTLINES (provided in class):   **OVERALL LETTER GRADE_____**

_____Communicate a sense of proportion and detail that is consistent with content

_____Provide enough information to assist the notetaking process without making taking notes unnecessary

_____Include space for students to write additional information

_____Are enhanced by lecture presentations in class

STUDY QUESTIONS/
REVIEW MATERIALS/
SAMPLE PROBLEMS: **OVERALL LETTER GRADE_____**

_____Prepare one to perform successfully on exams

_____Cover content that is covered on the exam

_____Are designed so that their completion makes the content easier to understand and remember

_____Do not focus on large quantities of material that are irrelevant to exam content

_____Provide enough opportunity to practice problem-solving skills

VISUAL MATERIALS
(as in prepared slides and transparencies):   **OVERALL LETTER GRADE_____**

_____Illustrate aspects of the content that are enhanced by visual representation

_____Are clear and "graphically" illustrate the content

_____Include written elaborations that are clear and easily read

_____Can be seen and read with ease everywhere in the classroom

_____Contain manageable amounts of material, so excessive amounts of time are not required to copy everything down

OVERALL CONCLUSIONS: (assign a letter grade to each item)

_____Grade these course materials compared with others you have used

_____Grade these materials in terms of how well they reflect this instructor's preparation and concern for students

SECTION FOUR

HOW
DO
YOU
TEACH?

FORM:
HOW DO YOU TEACH?

Encountering the Instructional Self

PURPOSE: Many instructors teach day after day but without a clear and accurate knowledge of what they do. If they had to describe their teaching in terms of the behaviors they use, most of the lists would be short. In part the problem results from the fact that, typically, descriptions of teaching are general and abstract. For example, research results repeatedly identify enthusiasm as one of the characteristics of effective instruction, but "enthusiasm" per se is an attitude, an internal state, something an instructor is. Until enthusiasm is described in terms of what someone who has it does, an instructor's ability to develop it is inhibited. The point is simple — instructors must be aware of their teaching behaviors, specifically and concretely. The premise is that implementing changes in teaching style is difficult if one is unaware of what one is changing from and to. This simple form aims to stimulate that sense of instructional awareness — for instructors to think about teaching strategies and style in terms of behaviors — what it is they "do" when they teach.

ADMINISTRATION: Administration is simple. Begin by carefully reading the items on the form. Are the answers to the questions known for sure? Absolutely? Do some questions cause hesitation? That may justify observation. Are there questions that cannot be answered? Note them. Over the next couple of days, try to discover the answers. Pay attention to teaching behaviors. Write reminders in the margins of lecture notes to stimulate observation in particular areas. Quite simply, work to become aware of teaching at this most mechanistic and fundamental level. And recognize it might take several days to discover all the answers.

INTERPRETATION: Interpretive concerns are not paramount to this endeavor. The goal is to discover the nuts and bolts that hold a particular teaching style together. The activity can be considered complete when an instructor is able to write a detailed description of his/her teaching style. Two tricks: the description can include "no" mention of content and "no" mention of physical characteristics like hair or eye color. The activity can be considered successful when the description is complete and accurate enough to allow identification of the instructor by someone else.

Recognize the almost automatic reaction of most instructors to judge behaviors. That is not the point now. Implicit in the questions on the form are not some pre-established criteria delineating what instructors ought to do. At this juncture, the objective is entirely descriptive. Discover what you do; then go about determining if it ought to be done differently.

Obviously, being aware of instructional behaviors is not the be-all and end-all of instructional development. Behaviors convey messages — important ones about attitudes, like enthusiasm, for example. So, instructors must, by various means, acquire input as to the impact of the behaviors they use. There are plenty of other forms in this catalogue designed especially to provide that input. But first, foremost, and most fundamentally, instructors must know how they teach.

SOURCE: This instrument was developed by the authors. It may be copied, altered, or adapted by instructors using the form to acquire instructional input.

HOW DO YOU TEACH?

1. WHAT DO YOU DO WITH YOUR HANDS? Gesture? Keep them in your pockets? Hold onto the podium? Play with the chalk? Hide them so students won't see them shake?

2. WHERE DO YOU STAND OR SIT? Behind the podium? On the table?

3. WHEN DO YOU MOVE TO A DIFFERENT LOCATION? Never? At regular ten-second intervals? When you change topics? When you need to write something on the board/overhead? When you answer a student's question? At what speed do you move? Do you talk and move at the same time?

4. WHERE DO YOU MOVE? Back behind the podium? Out to the students? To the blackboard?

5. WHERE DO YOUR EYES MOST OFTEN FOCUS? On your notes? On the board/overhead? Out the window? On a spot on the wall in the back of the classroom? On the students? Could you tell who was in class today without having taken roll?

6. WHAT DO YOU DO WHEN YOU FINISH ONE CONTENT SEGMENT AND ARE READY TO MOVE ON TO THE NEXT? Say OK? Ask if there are any questions? Erase the board? Move to a different location? Make a verbal transition?

7. WHEN DO YOU SPEAK LOUDER/SOFTER? When the point is very important? When nobody seems to understand? When nobody seems to be listening?

8. WHEN DO YOU SPEAK FASTER/SLOWER? When an idea is important and you want emphasize it? When you are behind where you ought to be on the content? When students are asking questions you're having trouble answering?

9. DO YOU LAUGH OR SMILE IN CLASS? When? How often?

10. HOW DO YOU USE EXAMPLES? How often do you include them? When do you include them?

11. HOW DO YOU EMPHASIZE MAIN POINTS? Write them on the board/overhead? Say them more than once? Ask the students if they understand them? Suggest ways they might be remembered?

12. WHAT DO YOU DO WHEN STUDENTS ARE INATTENTIVE? Ignore them? Stop and ask questions? Interject an anecdote? Point out the consequences of not paying attention? Move out toward them?

13. DO YOU ENCOURAGE STUDENT PARTICIPATION? How? Do you call on students by name? Do you grade it? Do you wait for answers? Do you verbally recognize quality contributions? Do you correct student answers? On a typical day, how much time is devoted to student talk?

14. HOW DO YOU BEGIN/END CLASS? With a summary and conclusion? With a preview and a review? With a gasp and a groan? With a bang and a whimper?

SECTION FIVE

INSTRUCTOR SELF EVALUATION

FORM:
INSTRUCTOR SELF-EVALUATION

PURPOSE: This instrument aims to provoke instructor reflection about assumptions and priorities that affect teaching. No set "right" answers exist nor are value judgments attached to a particular score. The goal is to encourage encounters with ideas and assumptions that inform the practice of instruction.

ADMINISTRATION: Instructors can complete this form at almost any juncture. Answers may be determined in terms of instructional activities in a given class or based on the general approach taken to teaching. The objective here is self-evaluation. The results need not be shared. For that reason, honesty is encouraged and really without risk.

INTERPRETATION: The last page of the instrument contains scoring instructions that ought to be consulted when the instrument has been completed. These interpretive suggestions should also be read then as well. **Do not read further if you intend to use this instrument.**
Scored results on this instrument identify areas of priority ascribed to one's teaching. Results should stimulate reflection and introspection. Are they what you anticipated or were you surprised by the results? Given a predilection towards a particular area, consider the instructional strategies and activities commonly included in your course. Do they communicate and reinforce this priority? What about the area on this instrument that represents the lowest priority? Should that area assume a greater importance? Are there instructional alterations that might increase your effectiveness in the area? Can they be implemented efficiently and without compromising your focus in other areas?
Burnout is a real, though often avoided, issue in academia. This instrument neither diagnoses its presence nor contains a solution. Would that the complicated dilemmas posed by psychological stress and fatigue could be identified and eradicated so easily! However, the instrument may serve as an early warning system or perhaps detect signs that burnout may be present. The place to look for this signal is not so much in the final scores but in the feelings experienced while filling out the form. If it was uniformly difficult to distinguish between items in a set, if the process of doing so sparked feelings of frustration, possibly followed by feelings of anger and ending with a general sense of not caring, the response may be indicative of burnout. Conclusions drawn must be tentative, but the ongoing stress associated with teaching course after course, year after year, ought not to be

overlooked or ignored. If nothing more, perhaps this form will encourage the recognition of the complexity associated with the act of teaching.

SOURCE: This instrument was developed by the Measurement and Research Division of the Office of Instructional Resources at the University of Illinois Urbana. It may be used in whole or part if credit is given to this source. Directions and scoring instructions have been revised by the authors of this volume. Interpretative suggestions were also added by these authors.

INSTRUCTOR SELF-EVALUATION FORM

Directions: Following are a number of statements describing aspects of college teaching. Examine the items in each set and rank them from 1 to 4 as to the degree to which they apply to your beliefs about teaching generally or your attitudes towards a course specifically. In responding, first examine the set and find the item that describes you or your course "most," and assign a rank of 1 to that statement. Then decide which statement describes you or your own course second-best; assign a rank of 2 to that item. Do likewise with the two remaining statements, assigning to them ranks of 3 and 4, respectively. If you find some items difficult to rank, show what your choice would be if you had to choose. It is important that you assign a different rank to each item and complete all sets in order to score the instrument.

SET 1

_____ a. I present thought-provoking ideas.

_____ b. I am sympathetic toward and considerate of students.

_____ c. I assist students in appreciating things they did not appreciate before.

_____ d. I am interested in and concerned with the quality of my teaching.

SET 2

_____ a. My students feel efforts made by them in the course are worthwhile.

_____ b. I am aware of students' needs.

_____ c. I raise challenging questions or problems in class.

_____ d. I make every effort to improve the quality of students' achievement in my course.

SET 3

_____ a. I encourage students to share in class their knowledge, opinions, and experiences.

_____ b. I help students become aware of the implications of the course's subject matter in their life.

_____ c. I remind students to come to me for help whenever it is needed.

_____ d. I analyze previous classroom experience to improve my teaching.

SET 4

_____a. I take an active, personal interest in improving my instruction.

_____b. I stimulate and answer questions in class.

_____c. I relate to students easily.

_____d. I help students to develop the ability to marshal or identify main points or central issues.

SET 5

_____a. I organize my course well.

_____b. I am knowledgeable about related areas aside from my own.

_____c. I stimulate students' appreciation for the subject.

_____d. I get along well with students.

SET 6

_____a. I restate questions or comments to clarify for the entire class.

_____b. I try to make every course the best every time.

_____c. I am sensitive to students' feelings.

_____d. I promote students' satisfaction in learning the subject matter.

SET 7

_____a. My students gain new viewpoints and appreciations.

_____b. I have zest and enthusiasm for teaching.

_____c. I develop a sense of mutual respect with students.

_____d. I present clear and relevant examples in class.

SET 8

_____a. I find teaching intellectually stimulating.

_____b. I make students feel at ease in conversations with me.

_____c. I stimulate students' interest in the subject.

_____d. I answer questions as thoroughly and precisely as possible.

SET 9

_____a. I coordinate different activities of my course well.

_____b. I look forward to class meetings.

_____ c. I enjoy having students come to me for consultation.

_____ d. My students feel that they can recognize good and poor reasoning or arguments in the field.

SET 10

_____ a. I try to function creatively in teaching my course.

_____ b. I encourage students to participate in class.

_____ c. I actively help students who are having difficulties.

_____ d. I stimulate students' intellectual curiosity.

SET 11

_____ a. I meet with students informally out of class when necessary.

_____ b. I make the objectives of the course clear.

_____ c. I try to make every course the best every time.

_____ d. My students become motivated to study and learn.

SCORING THE INSTRUCTOR SELF-EVALUATION FORM

The form has four scales. One statement from each set is associated with each scale.
Adequacy of Classroom Procedures
Enthusiasm for Teaching and Knowledge of Subject Matter
Stimulation of Cognitive and Affective Gains in Students
Relations with Students

STEP 1: Record the score assigned each individual item in each of the four areas.

STEP 2: Total each scale's scores.

ADEQUACY SCALE		ENTHUSIASM SCALE		STIMULATION SCALE		RELATIONS SCALE	
Set	1-a	Set	1-d	Set	1-c	Set	1-b
	2-c		2-d		2-a		2-b
	3-a		3-d		3-b		3-c
	4-b		4-a		4-d		4-c
	5-a		5-b		5-c		5-d
	6-a		6-b		6-d		6-c
	7-d		7-b		7-a		7-c
	8-d		8-a		8-c		8-b
	9-a		9-b		9-d		9-c
	10-b		10-a		10-d		10-c
	11-b		11-c		11-d		11-a
	TOTAL:		TOTAL:		TOTAL:		TOTAL:

STEP 3:   To interpret the results, consider the lowest total score to represent the area in this course or in your teaching generally to which you ascribe the highest priority. The cover sheet on the instrument contains some pointers on interpreting the results.

SECTION SIX

MADE-TO-ORDER FORM FOR INSTRUCTIONAL OBSERVATION
(Peer Version)

FORM:
MADE-TO-ORDER INSTRUCTIONAL OBSERVATION FORM *(Peer Version)*

PURPOSE: Colleagues can make substantive contributions to efforts to improve instruction, but they seldom do. Part of the problem is that typically classroom visitations occur as part of a promotion and tenure review. On those occasions, the visits precipitate some trepidation. However, what is proposed here incorporates colleague input in efforts to make instruction more effective, independent of the promotion and tenure process. Colleagues can do that if they are asked to provide feedback about the effects of specific aspects of instruction. Those aspects ought to represent areas of interest to the instructor and the attached instrument allows for the design of a form to represent those interests. The instructor selects and assembles items that are shared with the colleague reviewer prior to a classroom visit. The purpose is to give the colleague a set of guidelines that will add focus and direction to the instructional observation.

ADMINISTRATION: Begin by spending time with the list of suggested items. Mark those of interest. Write others that may not appear on the list. Assemble the selected items on the blank form provided, organizing them in the categories appearing on the list. Be realistic as to the number of items a colleague can carefully observe during a given class. If the items selected exceed the spaces provided, that may indicate the need for a second or follow-up visit.

Share the assembled instrument with the colleague doing the observation prior to the scheduled visitation. Providing relevant background can be useful — Why are these areas of interest? What precisely would you like to know about them? Encourage the colleague to fill out the form and make notes where appropriate. Consider completing a copy of the instrument yourself after the colleague observation. This provides a good point of comparison with colleague data.

INTERPRETATION: Plan to discuss the observation and completed form with the colleague. The point is not to make the colleague defend an assessment — everyone has a right to his or her opinion. The point for the instructor is to understand how and why the colleague came to the conclusion. Sometimes assessments of teaching are hard to understand — especially in terms of deciding what to do differently based on the assessment. That is because teaching is typically described in very abstract ways. The problem can be alleviated if the talk about teaching focuses on behaviors. If the colleague says, "Your teaching lacks enthusiasm," don't quarrel with the conclusion; rather find out what it is you do (or don't do) that caused the colleague to so conclude.

Be sure always to take colleague comments in context. This assessment of your teaching is based on the conclusions of one observer. That another observer would conclude the same thing can only be known for sure by asking. In fact, there is some research evidence indicating that colleague assessments of the same instructor do not often agree. The colleague is entitled to his or her opinion, but not to any claims of absolute truth.

Moreover, a colleague's comments are based on a small slice of a total teaching performance. How representative are they? Is this in fact the way you teach everyday in every class? Answers to those questions may not be known for certain, but the representativness of colleague assessments must be considered.

SOURCE: This instrument was developed by the authors. It may be copied, altered, and adapted by instructors using the form to acquire instructional input.

A Made-to-Order Form for Instructional Observation
(Peer Version)

ORGANIZATION

- [ ] Begins class on time in an orderly, organized fashion
- [ ] Previews lecture/discussion content
- [ ] Clearly states the goal or objective for the period
- [ ] Reviews prior class material to prepare students for the content to be covered
- [ ] Provides internal summaries and transitions
- [ ] Does not digress often from the main topic
- [ ] Summarizes and distills main points at the end of class
- [ ] Appears well-prepared for class

PRESENTATION

- [ ] Incorporates various instructional supports like slides, films, diagrams, etc.
- [ ] Uses instructional support effectively
- [ ] Responds to changes in student attentiveness
- [ ] Uses a variety of spaces in the classroom from which to present material (i.e., does not "hide" behind the podium)
- [ ] Blackboard writing is large and legible
- [ ] Speech fillers, (for example, "OK, ahm") are not distracting
- [ ] Speaks audibly and clearly
- [ ] Uses gestures to enhance meaning and not to release nervous tension (repetitive gestures tend to do the latter)
- [ ] Communicates a sense of enthusiasm and excitement toward the content
- [ ] Use of humor is positive and appropriate
- [ ] Presentation style facilitates note-taking
- [ ] Speech is neither too formal nor too casual
- [ ] Establishes and maintains eye contact with students

☐ Talks to the students, not the board or windows

☐ Varies the pace to keep students alert

☐ Selects teaching methods appropriate for the content

RAPPORT

☐ Praises students for contributions that deserve commendation

☐ Solicits student feedback

☐ Requires student thought and participation

☐ Responds constructively to student opinions

☐ Knows and uses student names

☐ Does not deprecate student ignorance or misunderstanding

☐ Responds to students as individuals

☐ Treats class members equitably

☐ Listens carefully to student comments and questions

☐ Tailors the course to help many kinds of students

☐ Recognizes when students do not understand

☐ Encourages mutual respect among students

☐ Credibility and control

☐ Responds to distractions effectively yet constructively

☐ Demonstrates content-competence

☐ Responds confidently to student inquiries for additional information

☐ Uses authority in classroom to create an environment conducive to learning

☐ Speaks about course content with confidence and authority

☐ Is able to admit error and/or insufficient knowledge

☐ Respects constructive criticism

CONTENT

☐ Includes illustrations

☐ Selects examples relevant to student experiences and course content

☐ Integrates text material into class presentations

☐ Relates current course content to what's gone before and will come after

☐ Relates current course content to students' general education

☐ Makes course content relevant with references to "real world" applications

☐ Presents views other than own when appropriate

☐ Seeks to apply theory to problem-solving

☐ Explicitly states relationships among various topics and facts/theory

☐ Explains difficult terms, concepts, or problems in more than one way

☐ Presents background of ideas and concepts

☐ Presents pertinent facts and concepts from related fields

☐ Presents up-to-date developments in the field

☐ Relates assignments to course content

☐ Clearly organizes assignments

☐ Carefully explains assignments

INTERACTION

☐ Encourages student questions, involvement, and debate

☐ Answers student questions clearly and directly

☐ Uses rhetorical questions to gain student attention

☐ Gives students enough time to respond to questions

☐ Refrains from answering own questions

☐ Responds to wrong answers constructively

☐ Allows ample time for questions

☐ Encourages students to respond to each other's questions

☐ Encourages students to answer difficult questions by providing cues and encouragement

☐ Allows relevant student discussion to proceed uninterrupted

☐ Presents challenging questions to stimulate discussion

☐ Respects diverse points of view

ACTIVE LEARNING (LABS, PE ACTIVITIES, ETC.)

☐ Clearly explains directions or procedures

☐ Clearly explains the goal of the activity

☐ Has readily available materials and equipment necessary to complete the activity

☐ Allows opportunity for individual expression

☐ Provides practice time

☐ Gives prompt attention to individual problems

☐ Provides individuals constructive verbal feedback

☐ Careful safety supervision is obvious

☐ Allows sufficient time for completion

☐ Provides enough demonstrations

☐ Demonstrations are clearly visible to all students

☐ If the discovery method is employed, schedules time for discussion of results

☐ Required skills are not beyond reasonable expectations for the course and/or students

☐ Provides opportunities for dialogue about the activity with peers and/or the instructor

☐ Allocates sufficient clean-up time within the class session

A Made-to-Order Form for Instructional Observation (Peer Version)

INSTRUCTIONS: Using the items below, identified by and discussed with the colleague you are observing, determine the general effectiveness of the faculty member for each item. Your mark on or somewhere between the distinctions "does well" and "needs improvement" should indicate that overall assessment. These general conclusions should be discussed with the faculty member involved. You should be able to explain your assessments with specific examples of what the instructor did or did not do to cause you to so conclude.

1. Organization

	Needs Improvement			Does Well
_____	— —	—	—	—
_____	— —	—	—	—
_____	— —	—	—	—
_____	— —	—	—	—
_____	— —	—	—	—
_____	— —	—	—	—

2. Presentation

_____	— —	—	—	—
_____	— —	—	—	—
_____	— —	—	—	—
_____	— —	—	—	—
_____	— —	—	—	—
_____	— —	—	—	—

3. Rapport

_____	— —	—	—	—
_____	— —	—	—	—
_____	— —	—	—	—
_____	— —	—	—	—
_____	— —	—	—	—
_____	— —	—	—	—

4. Content   Needs   Does
                                                 Improvement   Well

_____   ___ ___ ___ ___ ___
_____   ___ ___ ___ ___ ___
_____   ___ ___ ___ ___ ___
_____   ___ ___ ___ ___ ___
_____   ___ ___ ___ ___ ___
_____   ___ ___ ___ ___ ___

5. Interaction

_____   ___ ___ ___ ___ ___
_____   ___ ___ ___ ___ ___
_____   ___ ___ ___ ___ ___
_____   ___ ___ ___ ___ ___
_____   ___ ___ ___ ___ ___
_____   ___ ___ ___ ___ ___

6. Active Learning

_____   ___ ___ ___ ___ ___
_____   ___ ___ ___ ___ ___
_____   ___ ___ ___ ___ ___
_____   ___ ___ ___ ___ ___
_____   ___ ___ ___ ___ ___

SECTION SEVEN

MADE-TO-ORDER FORM FOR INSTRUCTIONAL OBSERVATION
(Student Version)

FORM:
MADE-TO-ORDER FORM FOR INSTRUCTIONAL OBSERVATION (Student Version)

PURPOSE: Students can tell professors what aspects of their teaching need improvement. The problem is that often instructors do not ask the right questions. This form solves that problem by letting students select the items to be assembled on the instrument. Groups of items (similar to those on the Peer Version of this form) are provided. Giving students this option also conveys a commitment to the value and propriety of the evaluation process.

Caveat: Despite instructions to the contrary, students may use this opportunity to assemble a collection of items that form a composite of everything an instructor does wrong. Do not overreact to the number of items where improvement might be indicated. This activity contains absolutely no guarantee that the assembled instrument represents a balanced depiction of the total teaching performance.

The point of the caveat is to caution instructors not to use data acquired in this way to support overall generalizations about the quality of instruction provided. Rather, the activity ought to be used as a means of getting input about aspects of instruction where one has never contemplated the presence of strengths or weaknesses.

ADMINISTRATION: This form will accomplish its stated purpose if students are given the opportunity to select the items. Probably the most expeditious means of accomplishing that is assigning the task to a small (5-7) student group, preferably composed of volunteers. If a large number of students indicate interest in the project, perhaps two instruments could be assembled and administered, either on different occasions or to different portions of the class. Encourage students to select only enough items to fill the two-page form. This way completion of the instrument will not consume exorbitant class time.

One suggestion for balancing the student perspective with that of the instructor is to have the students select three items from each of the general areas and have the instructor select the other three items. This technique might encourage a more balanced assessment and, in addition, has the advantage of giving the instructor the opportunity to ask students questions of particular interest.

When having the students complete the form, make sure they understand its origin. Encourage them to add comments proposing specific suggestions for improvement — or query the class generally about the propriety of the items selected — or offer them the opportunity to add evaluative items they wish had been included on the form.

INTERPRETATION: As already intimated, general conclusions are not really appropriate outcomes of this evaluative endeavor. Rather, the activity ought to be used as an idea source and eye-opener. The representativeness of the results can in part be determined by using the preceding Peer Version of the form or some other empirically tested instrument. Those comparisons will help put those data in perspective.

Means can be calculated for individual items. They should not be computed across items in an individual area. Probably of more value than calculating means is simply recording the number of responses for each given rank of the scale. That will clearly show the distribution of answers, which will also give hints as to their representativeness.

If results are confusing, if it is unclear what ought to be done about them, that ought to be discussed with the class. Evaluation activities like this provide excellent opportunities to open communication channels about a course. Maybe what offends or frustrates students cannot be changed, but it can always be discussed.

SOURCE: This instrument was developed by the authors. It may be copied, altered, or adapted by instructors using the form to acquire instructional input.

A Made-to-Order Form for Instructional Observation (Student Version)

Instructions: From the list below, select items that will provide your instructor with the most useful feedback. Research has shown that the most effective feedback is both positive and negative. This means the items you select ought to include both instructor behaviors that need improvement and those that are done well. Your instructor will assemble the selected items on the attached instrument. This evaluation form will then be completed by the class.

ORGANIZATION

☐ Begins class on time in an orderly, organized fashion

☐ Previews lecture/discussion content

☐ Clearly states the goal or objective for the period

☐ Reviews prior class material in preparation for the content to be covered

☐ Provides internal summaries and transitions

☐ Does not digress often from the main topic

☐ Summarizes and distills main points at the end of class

☐ Appears well-prepared for class

PRESENTATION

☐ Incorporates various instructional supports, e.g., slides, films, diagrams, etc.

☐ Uses a variety of spaces in the classroom from which to present material (i.e. does not "hide" behind the podium)

☐ Blackboard writing is large and legible

☐ Speech fillers, for example, ("OK, ahm") are not distracting

☐ Speaks audibly and clearly

☐ Use of gestures is positive, not annoying

☐ Communicates enthusiasm and excitement toward the content

☐ Use of humor is positive and appropriate

☐ Lectures are easy to take notes from

☐ Difficult vocabulary is explained

☐ Level of language is appropriate

☐ Talks to the students, not the board or windows

☐ Varies the pace

☐ Does not speak in a monotone

RAPPORT

- ☐ Acknowledges deserving student contributions
- ☐ Solicits feedback
- ☐ Requires student thought and participation
- ☐ Responds constructively to student opinions
- ☐ Knows and uses student names
- ☐ Does not deprecate ignorance or misunderstanding
- ☐ Responds to students as individuals
- ☐ Treats class members equitably
- ☐ Listens carefully to comments and questions
- ☐ Recognizes when students do not understand or are confused
- ☐ Encourages mutual respect among students

CREDIBILITY AND CONTROL

- ☐ Responds to distractions effectively yet constructively
- ☐ Appears comfortable and competent with the content
- ☐ Responds confidently to student inquiries for additional information
- ☐ Uses authority in the classroom to create an environment conducive to learning
- ☐ Speaks about course content with confidence and authority
- ☐ Is able to admit error and/or insufficient knowledge
- ☐ Respects constructive criticism

CONTENT

☐ Includes illustrations

☐ Selects examples relevant to student experiences and course content

☐ Integrates text material into class presentations

☐ Relates current course content to what's gone before and will come after

☐ Relates current course content to students' general education

☐ Makes course content relevant with references to "real world" applications

☐ Presents views other than own

☐ Seeks to apply theory to problem-solving

☐ Helps students understand relationships among various topics and facts/theory

☐ Explains difficult concepts or problems in more than one way

☐ Presents background of ideas and concepts

☐ Presents pertinent facts and concepts from related fields

☐ Presents up-to-date developments in the field

☐ Relates assignments to course content

☐ Clearly organizes assignments

☐ Carefully explains assignments

INTERACTION

☐ Encourages questions, involvement, and debate

☐ Answers questions clearly and directly

☐ Uses rhetorical questions to gain attention

☐ Provides enough time for students to respond to questions

☐ Refrains from answering own questions

☐ Responds to wrong answers constructively

☐ Provides ample time in which students may ask questions

☐ Encourages students to respond to each other's questions

☐ Encourages students to answer difficult questions by providing cues and encouragement

☐ Allows relevant student discussion to proceed uninterrupted

☐ Presents challenging questions to stimulate discussion

☐ Respects diverse points of view

ACTIVE LEARNING (items especially relevant to labs, PE activities, etc.)

☐ Clearly explains directions or procedures

☐ Clearly explains the goal of the activity

☐ Has readily available the materials and equipment necessary to complete the activity

☐ Allows opportunity for individual expression

☐ Provides practice time

☐ Gives prompt attention to individual problems

☐ Provides individuals constructive verbal feedback

☐ Careful safety supervision is obvious

☐ Allows sufficient time for completion

☐ Provides enough demonstrations

☐ Demonstrations are clearly visible to everyone

☐ If the discovery method is employed, schedules time for discussion of results

☐ Required skills are not beyond reasonable expectations for the course and/or students

☐ Provides opportunities for dialogue about the activity with classmates and/or the instructor

☐ Allocates sufficient clean-up time within the class session

A CLASS-ASSEMBLED INSTRUCTIONAL EVALUATION

INSTRUCTIONS: Members of this class have selected the areas and the items that appear on this evaluation form. This means your instructor not only cares enough to solicit input but has gone a step further and allowed students to identify areas and items on that his or her instructional effectiveness should be judged. Please do your part by providing careful and thoughtful responses to the items provided. Indicate your evaluation by marking X on the scale at the position you deem appropriate.

1. Organization

Needs Improvement   Does Well

_____   ___ ___ ___ ___ ___

_____   ___ ___ ___ ___ ___

_____   ___ ___ ___ ___ ___

_____   ___ ___ ___ ___ ___

_____   ___ ___ ___ ___ ___

_____   ___ ___ ___ ___ ___

2. Presentation

_____   ___ ___ ___ ___ ___

_____   ___ ___ ___ ___ ___

_____   ___ ___ ___ ___ ___

_____   ___ ___ ___ ___ ___

_____   ___ ___ ___ ___ ___

_____   ___ ___ ___ ___ ___

3. Rapport

_____   ___ ___ ___ ___ ___

_____   ___ ___ ___ ___ ___

_____   ___ ___ ___ ___ ___

_____   ___ ___ ___ ___ ___

_____   ___ ___ ___ ___ ___

_____   ___ ___ ___ ___ ___

4. Credibility & Control

Needs Improvement

Does Well

_____

_____

_____

_____

_____

_____

5. Content

_____

_____

_____

_____

_____

_____

6. Interaction

_____

_____

_____

_____

_____

_____

7. Active Learning

_____

_____

_____

_____

_____

_____

SECTION EIGHT

OPEN
ENDED
QUESTIONNAIRE

FORM:
OPEN-ENDED QUESTIONAIRE

PURPOSE: Open-ended questions provide a plethora of data about instruction. They should be used as sources of ideas, providers of detail, and pinpointers of problems.

ADMINISTRATION: The first and most important administrative issue involves phrasing open-ended questions. The principal problem with open-ended items is that they can be phrased so that they are too open. In that case, the data can be of less than substantive value. A question like, "What did you like most about the course?" can generate responses like, "The professor's pink shirt" as well as observations like, "The way the professor used personal examples." However, questions can be focused in ways that make it difficult for students to contribute irrelevant and sometimes irresponsible comments. Examples on the following page illustrate that focus.

The problem of inappropriate comments can also be diminished by personally requesting responses from a select group of students. Clearly, the procedure of selecting students must be used carefully. Requesting input from only those students doing well in the course will skew the perspective in much the same way requesting response from only those doing poorly will skew it oppositely. The goal is a balanced perspective, identifying students who will give careful thought to the questions and letting any student who sincerely wants to provide input the opportunity to do so.

Open-ended questions are not well-suited to hastily conceived answers penned in the final few minutes of class. Encourage students to take the forms home and fill them out after some thoughtful reflection. Yes, some will never be returned, but the goal with open-ended evaluation is the quality, not the quantity of responses. Also, the quality of student response will increase if they know the instructor is seriously interested in their input, plans to discuss the results with them, and is willing to implement appropriate alterations.

The attached questions illustrate a variety of open-ended question options. They overlap, and there are too many to expect students to respond to all of them. The advice is to make selections, revise if need be, and assemble enough open-ended queries to fill one page, leaving five or six lines for each response. If the class is large and more than five or six of the questions are of interest, construct two forms, distributing the different versions throughout the class.

INTERPRETATION: Data from open-ended questions are difficult to manage. If the class is large, the task is also time-consuming. The assessments offered are never worded exactly the same way, which makes tabulation an activity of approximation at best. However, recall what function open-ended questionnaires best fill — idea source. Review responses with that in mind and look for major trends. Perspectives on results can also be gained by sharing student answers with an objective outsider, like a trusted colleague. Ask the colleague what he or she might consider changing if he or she had received these evaluative responses.

SOURCE: The attached questions are adapted, elaborated, and revised from a set offered by Noel McInnis in an article, "How to Know What to Self Renew" in *Implementing Innovative Instruction*, published in Spring 1974.

OPEN-ENDED QUESTIONNAIRE

Instructions: This evaluation form is designed to produce information about the instruction that will make it easier to determine what, if any, changes need to be made. Your thoughtful and complete response will be most appreciated. Responses that include specific examples and illustrations will provide the most useful data. You need not sign the form. Return it the next class session or any time during the next couple of days. Proposed changes, based on responses provided here, will be discussed with the class prior to their implementation.

When do you find the instructor *most* helpful in your learning?
When do you find the instructor *least* helpful in your learning?

When do you find the instructor making himself or herself *most* clearly understood?
When do you find the instructor making himself or herself *least* clearly understood?

When do you feel *most* intellectually stimulated by this course?
When do you feel *least* intellectually stimulated by this course?

When are you *clearest* about what material ought to be in your notes?
When are you *confused* about what material ought to be in your notes?

When do you feel *most* convinced that the course is worth your effort?
When do you feel *least* convinced that the course is worth your effort?

When do you feel *most* certain that the instructor cares whether you succeed in the course?
When do you feel *least* certain that the instructor cares whether you succeed in the course?

When do you feel *most* sure that you understand course objectives?
When do you feel *least* sure that you understand course objectives?

When do you *most* want to discuss the material in this course?
When do you *least* want to discuss the material in this course?

When do you find yourself listening *most* intently to lecture material in this course?
When do you find yourself listening *least* intently to lecture material in this course?

Which assignments/class activities are *most* relevant to course objectives and student needs?
Which assignments/class activities are *least* relevant to course objectives and student needs?

SECTION NINE

SELF- OR COLLEAGUE-ANALYSIS OF VIDEOTAPED TEACHING SAMPLE

FORM:
SELF OR COLLEAGUE ANALYSIS OF VIDEOTAPED TEACHING SAMPLE

PURPOSE: Videotape is without doubt one of the most effective mediums for improving instruction. It is also one of the most anxiety-provoking. It is all well and good to have students assess aspects of instruction, even on occasion to have colleagues offer comments, but to confront the teaching self on tape is quite another story. Generally what happens first is that the instructor focuses on physical characteristics: Do I look that old? Why is my hair sticking up in the back? Where did that arm gesture come from? The purpose of this form is to move the focus away from those areas to the more substantive aspects of teaching. It can serve to guide the review of a taped teaching sample.

ADMINISTRATION: The form can be used for a self-analysis of videotaped teaching or by a colleague reviewer. It is probably most effective if it is used by both and discussed jointly. The problem with self-review is objectivity — reaching a place distant enough so that teaching can be viewed dispassionately. A colleague can help a faculty member reach that place by pointing out teaching behaviors that might otherwise be missed.

Instructors using this instructional development strategy are advised to wait at least a day or so after taping before viewing the tape. The instructor and colleague can look at the tape separately or together. Either way, the discussion that follows will have a greater effect if the conclusions offered can be illustrated with examples on the tape. If, for example, the colleague believes the instructor does not summarize content segments adequately, points of transition on the tape can be viewed jointly and what the instructor does or does not do can be seen. This is one of the advantages of videotape analysis — it is difficult to argue about whether or not a particular behavior occurred.

INTERPRETATION: Obviously, tabulating the results recorded on this form is not especially important. The ratings of the instructor and colleague can be compared to identify areas of disagreements, which can then be discussed and reviewed, if need be. It is also important to see the behaviors in context, meaning, that the instructor's goals (both immediate and long term) are relevant. What has gone before in the class and what will come after will have an effect, and who the students are makes a difference. A colleague reviewer ought to offer assessments apprised of this context. Moreover, generalizations from the tape ought to be modest in scope. A 20-minute teaching sample is representative, but *how* representative is a crucial consideration. In terms of a total teaching performance spanning 15 weeks in a course, three different courses in a semester, 10 different courses during four years, it is at best a small slice. Finally, the act of being taped has effects. Most instructors feel the presence of the camera. How does that awareness effect what they do? The question has no definite answer, but the affect of being taped needs to be taken into account.

SOURCE: Diamond, N., Sharp, G., and Ory, J. C. *Improving Your Lecturing*, Urbana: Office of Instructional Resources, University of Illinois, 1978. The instrument may be used in whole or part if credit is given the source.

Self- or Colleague-Analysis of Videotaped Teaching Sample

Directions: Respond to each of the statements below by circling the number that most closely corresponds to your observation.

3 = Very Satisfied
2 = Satisfied
1 = Needs Improvement
NA = Not Applicable

IMPORTANCE AND SUITABILITY OF CONTENT

1. The material presented is generally accepted by colleagues to be worth knowing.   3   2   1   NA

2. The material presented is important for this group of students.   3   2   1   NA

3. Students seem to have the necessary background to understand the material.   3   2   1   NA

4. The examples used drew upon students' experiences.   3   2   1   NA

5. When appropriate, a distinction was made between factual material and opinions.   3   2   1   NA

6. When appropriate, authorities were cited to support statements.   3   2   1   NA

7. When appropriate, divergent viewpoints were presented.   3   2   1   NA

8. A sufficient amount of material was included in the lecture.   3   2   1   NA

ORGANIZATION OF CONTENT

Introductory Portion

1. Stated the purpose of the lecture.   3   2   1   NA

2. Presented a brief overview of the lecture content.   3   2   1   NA

3. Stated a problem to be solved or discussed during the lecture.   3   2   1   NA

4. Discussed the relationship between this and previous lectures.   3   2   1   NA

Body of Lecture

5. Arranged and discussed the content in a systematic and organized fashion that was made explicit to the students.　　3　2　1　NA

6. Asked questions periodically to determine if too much or too little information was being presented.　　3　2　1　NA

7. Presented examples to clarify very abstract and difficult ideas.　　3　2　1　NA

8. Explicitly stated the relationships among various ideas in the lecture.　　3　2　1　NA

9. Periodically summarized the most important ideas in the lecture.　　3　2　1　NA

Conclusion of Lecture

10. Summarized the main ideas in the lecture.　　3　2　1　NA

11. Solved or otherwise dealt with any problems.　　3　2　1　NA

12. Related the day's lecture to upcoming presentations.　　3　2　1　NA

13. Restated what students were expected to gain from the lecture material.　　3　2　1　NA

PRESENTATION STYLE

Voice Characteristics

1. Voice could be easily heard.　　3　2　1　NA

2. Voice was raised or lowered for variety and emphasis.　　3　2　1　NA

3. Speech was neither too formal nor too casual.　　3　2　1　NA

4. Speech fillers, for example, "OK now," "ahmm," etc., were not distracting.　　3　2　1　NA

5. Rate of speech was neither too fast nor too slow.　　3　2　1　NA

Nonverbal Communication

6. Established and maintained eye contact with the class.　　3　2　1　NA

7. Listened carefully to student comments and questions.　　3　2　1　NA

8. Wasn't too stiff and formal in appearance.　　3　2　1　NA

9. Wasn't too casual in appearance.	3	2	1	NA

10. Facial and bodily movements did not contradict speech or expressed intentions. (For example, waited for responses after asking questions.)	3	2	1	NA

Clarity of Presentation

1. Stated purpose at the beginning of the lecture.   3   2   1   NA

2. Defined new terms, concepts, and principles.   3   2   1   NA

3. Used relevant, clear, and simple examples to explain major ideas.   3   2   1   NA

4. Explicitly related new ideas to already familiar ones.   3   2   1   NA

5. Reiterated definitions of new terms to help students become accustomed to them.   3   2   1   NA

6. Provided occasional summaries and restatements of important ideas.   3   2   1   NA

7. Used alternative explanations when necessary.   3   2   1   NA

8. Slowed the word flow when ideas were complex and difficult.   3   2   1   NA

9. Did not often digress from the main topic.   3   2   1   NA

10. Talked to the students, not to the board or windows.   3   2   1   NA

11. The board work appeared organized and legible.   3   2   1   NA

ESTABLISHING AND MAINTAINING CONTACT WITH STUDENTS

Establishing Contact

1. Greeted students with a bit of small talk.   3   2   1   NA

2. Established eye contact with as many students as possible.   3   2   1   NA

3. Used questions to gain student attention.   3   2   1   NA

4. Encouraged student questions.   3   2   1   NA

Maintaining Contact

5. Asked questions that allowed the instructor to gauge student progress.   3   2   1   NA

6. Noted and responded to signs of puzzlement, boredom, curiosity, and so on.   3   2   1   NA

7. Varied the pace of the lecture to keep students alert.   3   2   1   NA

8. Spoke at a rate that allowed students time to take notes.   3   2   1   NA

Questioning Ability

1. Asked questions to see what the students knew about the topic.   3   2   1   NA

2. Addressed questions to individual students as well as the group at large.   3   2   1   NA

3. Used rhetorical questions to gain students' attention.   3   2   1   NA

4. Paused after all questions to allow students time to think of an answer.   3   2   1   NA

5. Encouraged students to answer difficult questions by providing cues or rephrasing.   3   2   1   NA

6. When necessary, asked students to clarify their questions.   3   2   1   NA

7. Asked probing questions if a student's answer was incomplete or superficial.   3   2   1   NA

8. Repeated answers when necessary so the entire class could hear.   3   2   1   NA

9. Received student questions politely and, when possible, enthusiastically.   3   2   1   NA

10. Refrained from answering questions when unsure of a correct response.   3   2   1   NA

SECTION TEN

SPECIFICALLY,
WHAT
NEEDS
IMPROVEMENT?
(Instructor Version)

FORM:
SPECIFICALLY, WHAT NEEDS IMPROVEMENT? *(Instructor Version)*

PURPOSE: Efforts to improve *teaching* ought to be met with efforts to improve *learning*. In other words, your activities to improve teaching techniques ought to occur publicly so students are aware, of the efforts and are encouraged by your example to consider their contributions to the overall health and well-being of the classroom climate. This form provides the opportunity to give students specific feedback about these contributions.

ADMINISTRATION: If students have participated in an evaluation activity offering you input about the instruction, the day you discuss that feedback and any decisions you've reached would be an excellent time to offer students information about their contributions to the overall classroom climate. Be aware that students are unaccustomed to receiving feedback like this. Apprise them of the objectives behind the activity — that classroom climates are created and affected by the contributions of everyone involved — not just the instructor. The form could be made into a transparency and actually filled out in front of the students. However the contents are shared, the communication needs to be constructive. Never address the behaviors of individuals; discuss only the generalized contributions of the class. If changes are desired, describe them in concrete terms. And if you subsequently see evidence of those changes, by all means commend them.

INTERPRETATION: Interpretation in this case means suggestions on filling out the form. Determine positions on the rating scale by comparing this particular class with previous ones or against a mental conception of the "ideal" class. Whatever the standard, it needs to be communicated to students. In preparing this feedback for students, the golden rule applies. Do unto students as you would have them do unto you when it comes to the kind of evaluation data offered.

SOURCE: This instrument was developed by the authors. It may be copied, altered, or adapted by instructors using the form to acquire instructional input.

WHAT NEEDS IMPROVEMENT?
Suggestions for students in _____

1. Visible evidence of student interest in the subject matter
   CLASS DOES WELL   CLASS NEEDS IMPROVEMENT

   ___   ___   ___   ___   ___

   Suggestions for demonstrating interest in the subject matter:

2. Vigorous in-class discussions
   CLASS DOES WELL   CLASS NEEDS IMPROVEMENT

   ___   ___   ___   ___   ___

   Suggestions for making class discussion more vigorous:

3. Levels of student participation
   CLASS DOES WELL   CLASS NEEDS IMPROVEMENT

   ___   ___   ___   ___   ___

   Suggestions for increasing student participation:

4. Indications of whether or not course content is understood
   CLASS DOES WELL   CLASS NEEDS IMPROVEMENT

   ___   ___   ___   ___   ___

   Suggestions for indicating course content:

5. Assuming initiative and responsibility for individual learning
   CLASS DOES WELL   CLASS NEEDS IMPROVEMENT

   ___   ___   ___   ___   ___

   Suggestions for assuming initiative and responsibility for learning:

6. Levels of attentiveness in class
   CLASS DOES WELL   CLASS NEEDS IMPROVEMENT

   ___   ___   ___   ___   ___

   Suggestions for increasing class attentiveness

7. Support and recognition of contributions made by others in the class
   CLASS DOES WELL   CLASS NEEDS IMPROVEMENT

   ___   ___   ___   ___   ___

   Suggestions for showing support and recognition of others:

8. Appropriate standards of academic integrity
   CLASS DOES WELL   CLASS NEEDS IMPROVEMENT

   ___   ___   ___   ___   ___

   Suggestions for raising standards of academic integrity:

9. Use of office hours, review sessions, and supplemenatry study aids
   CLASS DOES WELL   CLASS NEEDS IMPROVEMENT

   ___   ___   ___   ___   ___

   Suggestions for using office hours, review sessions, and supplementary study aids:

SECTION ELEVEN

SPECIFICALLY,
WHAT
NEEDS
IMPROVEMENT?
(*Student Version*)

FORM:
SPECIFICALLY, WHAT NEEDS IMPROVEMENT? (Student Version)

PURPOSE: This instrument is designed to identify areas where improvement efforts might be focused. Instructors who want specific guidance as to areas where changes ought to be implemented should consider this form. It is a good follow-up to a diagnostic instrument which may raise some questions about specific aspects of instruction. Data from this instrument can help fill in details that may be missing.

Caveat: This form assumes that the instruction offered needs improvement. The form is not, however, based on premises of deficiency. It assumes, rather, that the quest for instructional effectiveness is an on-going endeavor, that teaching is ever in need of refinement.

ADMINISTRATION: If the form is to be completed conscientiously, that will take time — at least 15 minutes. Perhaps the form can be distributed to students to complete at home. Granted, not as many will be returned, but those that are returned are likely to have been completed conscientiously. Quality student response is also likely to be a function of instructor communication to the class about the activity. Be forthright and open. You are requesting this information because you want to know. You will give careful consideration to the suggestions offered. Let students know you appreciate the time and effort they will take to provide input.

Caveat: The form may include aspects entirely irrelevant to your instructional situation. Those items can be deleted; others of interest and value that have been omitted can be added. Alter and adapt the instrument as need be.

INTERPRETATION: Calculate the means for each item. Notice the extent of agreement for a given answer. It makes a difference if the mean is 5 and every answer falls between 4 and 6, or if the mean is 5 and answers chosen have a larger variation. In this second situation, one concludes that a particular aspect of instruction is having mixed effects on students. Implementing changes ought to occur carefully; otherwise, the mean might well remain the same and only the students pleased and displeased change.

Look upon the suggestions offered as a source of ideas, not a mandate for what must be done. Keep a running tally of how often the same suggestion occurs. Again that does not necessarily prescribe what must be done — only the student perception of a cure. Perhaps that remedy won't work; perhaps it will. Either way, their suggestions ought to be taken seriously and, whatever you decide, discuss the conclusions with them.

SOURCE: The list of items on the form is drawn from a survey instrument used in a 1978 Project on Institutional Renewal through the Improvement of Teaching. The survey identified aspects of instruction students felt were most in need of improvement. The instruction design and format are a product of the authors. It may be copied by instructors using the form to acquire instructional input.

SPECIFICALLY, WHAT NEEDS IMPROVEMENT?

INSTRUCTIONS: Help your instructor identify areas where efforts to make this course better ought to focus. Specific recommendations for changes in the area can be indicated in the space provided. Please answer and make recommendations recognizing that certain limitations (like class size and meeting time) may be imposed on the instructor by campus authorities.

1. Stimulates interest of the students in the subject matter
   CLASS DOES WELL   CLASS NEEDS IMPROVEMENT

   ___   ___   ___   ___   ___

   Suggestions for stimulating interest:

2. Exhibits knowledge of the subject matter
   CLASS DOES WELL   CLASS NEEDS IMPROVEMENT

   ___   ___   ___   ___   ___

   Areas in which the instructor needs to be more knowledgeable:

3. Encourages more vigorous class discussions
   CLASS DOES WELL   CLASS NEEDS IMPROVEMENT

   ___   ___   ___   ___   ___

   Suggestions for encouraging discussion:

4. Conveys enthusiasm for the course
   CLASS DOES WELL   CLASS NEEDS IMPROVEMENT

   ___   ___   ___   ___   ___

   Suggestions for conveying enthusiasm:

5. Individualizes instruction for self-paced study
   CLASS DOES WELL   CLASS NEEDS IMPROVEMENT

   ___   ___   ___   ___   ___

   Ways instruction might be individualized:

6. Relates the subject matter more to student interests and experiences
   CLASS DOES WELL   CLASS NEEDS IMPROVEMENT

   ___   ___   ___   ___   ___

   Suggestions for relating subject to student interests and experiences:

7. Provides opportunities for non-classroom learning
   CLASS DOES WELL   CLASS NEEDS IMPROVEMENT

   ___   ___   ___   ___   ___

   Examples of appropriate non-classroom learning opportunities:

8. Uses media and technology in the course
   CLASS DOES WELL   CLASS NEEDS IMPROVEMENT

   ___   ___   ___   ___   ___

   Examples of ways media and technology might be incorporated in the course:

9. Clarifies course objectives
CLASS DOES WELL   CLASS NEEDS IMPROVEMENT

___   ___   ___   ___   ___

Suggestions for clarifying course objectives:

10. Sets and maintains appropriate academic standards in the course
CLASS DOES WELL   CLASS NEEDS IMPROVEMENT

___   ___   ___   ___   ___

Suggests what standards ought to be raised (or lowered, if that's the problem):

11. Includes student participation in setting course goals
CLASS DOES WELL   CLASS NEEDS IMPROVEMENT

___   ___   ___   ___   ___

Suggestions for increasing student participation:

12. Fairness of testing and grading policies and practices
CLASS DOES WELL   CLASS NEEDS IMPROVEMENT

___   ___   ___   ___   ___

Suggestions for improving testing and grading:

13. Treats students as adults
CLASS DOES WELL   CLASS NEEDS IMPROVEMENT

___   ___   ___   ___   ___

Ways to improve treatment of students:

14. Presentation skills of the instructor
    CLASS DOES WELL   CLASS NEEDS IMPROVEMENT

    ——   ——   ——   ——   ——

    Suggestions for improving presentational skills:

15. Provides course assignments and out-of-class activities
    CLASS DOES WELL   CLASS NEEDS IMPROVEMENT

    ——   ——   ——   ——   ——

    Ways to improve course assignments and out-of-class activities:

SECTION TWELVE

TEACHER
BEHAVIORS
INVENTORY

FORM:
TEACHER BEHAVIORS INVENTORY

PURPOSE: Very often evaluation instruments do not describe effective instruction concretely. They focus on what effective instructors "are like" — enthusiastic, friendly, accessible — as opposed to what those who teach "do." The distinction is an important one because if you are interested in improving your performance in the classroom, it is much more helpful to identify what you are "doing" instead of what you should "be." The Teacher Behaviors Inventory makes an important contribution in this area. The developer, H.G. Murray, of this instrument reviewed research that attempts to identify some of the components of effective instruction. He then hypothesized what teaching behaviors might be associated with those components. A collection of those behaviors appears on the inventory that follows. In subsequent research, Murray found that a number of the behaviors on the inventory did correlate significantly with student ratings of overall instructor effectiveness.

Because the items on this form describe behaviors, it will provide input that focuses more on the "presentational" aspects of instruction than on the "content." This does not mean that content competence should be ruled out as an ingredient of effective instruction — only that the focus here is more on the processes of instruction. This behavioral orientation makes this form especially well-suited to courses where the lecture or lecture-discussion method is used to present content.

ADMINISTRATION: Have students complete the form in class, allowing approximately 15 minutes for its administration. Before distributing the form, spend a few minutes telling students why you are interested in this feedback and how you intend to use it.

INTERPRETATION: Calculate means and standard deviations for each of the individual items, noting the extent of agreement among students as indicated by the standard deviation. If the standard deviation for the responses of one of the items is large, this may indicate a need to discuss the item with the students to see if they can explain their different responses. This instrument does not lend itself well to overall averaging of the item means, as there are negatively worded items included. The instrument works well in documenting progress that may be part of an instructional improvement effort that extends across a number of semesters. Two or three behaviors can be targeted for improvement and the results of those efforts monitored regularly with this form.

SOURCE: This inventory was developed by H. G. Murray, Department of Psychology, University of Western Ontario. It is not copyrighted and may be reproduced for any valid research or instructional development purpose.

TEACHERS BEHAVIORS INVENTORY

INSTRUCTIONS: In this inventory you are asked to assess your instructor's specific classroom behaviors. Your instructor has requested this information for purposes of instructional analysis and improvement. Please try to be both thoughtful and candid in your responses, so as to maximize the value of feedback.

Your judgments should reflect that type of teaching you think is best for this particular course and your particular learning style. Try to assess each behavior independently, rather than letting your overall impression of the instructor determine each individual rating.

Each section of the inventory begins with a definition of the category of teaching to be assessed in that section. For each specific teaching behavior, please indicate your judgment as to the frequency your instructor exhibits the behavior in question. Please use the following rating scale in making your judgments:

TEACHER BEHAVIORS INVENTORY					
	1 ALMOST NEVER	2 RARELY	3 SOMETIMES	4 OFTEN	5 ALMOST ALWAYS
CLARITY: methods used to explain or clarify concepts and principles					
Gives several examples of each concept					
Uses concrete everyday examples to explain concepts and principles					
Fails to define new or unfamiliar terms					
Repeats difficult ideas several times					
Stresses most important points by pausing, speaking slowly, raising voice, and so on					
Uses graphs or diagrams to facilitate explanation					
Points out practical applications of concepts					
Answers students' questions thoroughly					
Suggests ways of memorizing complicated ideas					

TEACHER BEHAVIORS INVENTORY					
	1 ALMOST NEVER	2 RARELY	3 SOMETIMES	4 OFTEN	5 ALMOST ALWAYS
Writes key terms on blackboard or overhead screen					
Explains subject matter in familiar colloquial language					
ENTHUSIASM: use of nonverbal behavior to solicit student attention and interest					
Speaks in a dramatic or expressive way					
Moves about while lecturing					
Gestures with hands or arms					
Exhibits facial gestures or expressions					
Avoids eye contact with students					
Walks up aisles beside students					
Gestures with head or body					
Tells jokes or humorous anecdotes					
Reads lecture verbatim from prepared notes or text					
Smiles or laughs while teaching					
Shows distracting mannerisms					
INTERACTION: techniques used to foster students participation in class					
Encourages students to ask questions or make comments during lectures					
Criticizes students when they make errors					
Praises students for good ideas					
Asks questions of individual students					
Asks questions of class as a whole					
Incorporates students' ideas into lecture					
Presents challenging, thought-provoking ideas					
Uses a variety of media and activities in class					
Asks rhetorical questions					

TEACHER BEHAVIORS INVENTORY					
	1 ALMOST NEVER	2 RARELY	3 SOMETIMES	4 OFTEN	5 ALMOST ALWAYS
ORGANIZATION: ways of organizing or structuring subject matter of course					
Uses headings and subheadings to organize lectures					
Puts outline of lecture on blackboard/overhead screen					
Clearly indicates transition from one topic to the next					
Gives preliminary overview of lecture at begining of class					
Periodically summarizes points previously made					
PACING: rate of presentation of information, efficient use fo class time					
Dwells excessively on obvious points					
Digresses from major theme of lecture					
Covers very little material in class sessions					
Asks if students understand before proceeding to next topic					
Sticks to the point in answering students' questions					
DISCLOSURE: explicitness concerning course requirements and grading criteria					
Advises students as to how to preapre for tests or exams					
Provides sample exam questions					
Tells students exactly what is expected of them on tests, essays, or assignments					
States objectives of each lecture					
Reminds students of test dates or assignment deadlines					
States objectives of course as a whole					
SPEECH: characteristics of voice relevant to classroom teaching					
Stutters, mumbles, or slurs words					
Speaks at an approriate volume					

TEACHER BEHAVIORS INVENTORY					
	1 **ALMOST NEVER**	2 **RARELY**	3 **SOMETIMES**	4 **OFTEN**	5 **ALMOST ALWAYS**
Speaks clearly					
Speaks at appropriate pace					
Says "um" or "ah"					
Voice lacks proper modulation (speaks in monotone)					
RAPPORT: quality of interpersonal relations between teacher and students					
Addresses individual students by name					
Announces availability for consultation outside of class					
Shows tolerance of other points of view					
Talks with students before or after class					